2840 West Rowena Avenue
Los Angeles, California 90039

hello! world

Lori Bard

HOUSTON PUBLIC LIBRARY

Copyright © 1970

Mara Books Incorporated
2840 West Rowena Avenue,
Los Angeles, California

Library of Congress number 71-124681

International Standard Book number 0-87787-001-2

to my mother
C'est parceque ma mère a bien travaillé

Prologue

Like all young people who had grown up on the American writers of the Lost Generation, I had a passion to live in Europe. At last, at the age of twenty-three, I made the voyage. I had taught elementary school for two years, which prepared me for anything! I had enough money to live like a student for a year or a human being for six months.

For several months before I left, I collected names and travel tips from everyone I encountered. I cornered people who had lived in Europe and wrote down everything they said. I wanted to go everywhere, see everything. To be "authentic" the trip must be by boat; I must cross personally each mile of the United States and the Atlantic.

Through a series of fortunate decisions I managed to stay for almost two years. A cousin gave me the name of a friend who worked on the Paris *Herald Tribune*. His wife taught at the American School. To satisfy my compelling need to stay in Paris I took her suggestion of tutoring American children waiting to get into the small school. When one of the faculty decided to leave I was right there to fill the vacancy.

After a couple of two-night train rides I knew I had to have a car. One morning I walked into the Renault agency on the Champs Elysées and said, "I want a yellow one." Even though the cost of the car dissolved many months of travel allowance, I knew the increased mobility was worth it.

The excitement of getting on the boat to France kept me awake several nights before sailing day. Was it really me? Was it really so easy to just go?

Contents

Prologue vii
Paris 1
Concièrge 7
Sion 15
Gard 19
Castelnou 25
Arvika 29
Fontainebleau 33
La Grande Chaumière 37
Lascaux 41
Tunis 45
Altamira 51
Belgrade 55
Train to Dubrovnik 59
Lokrum 65
Trebenje 69
Zagreb-Athens 75
Iraklion 79
Crete 85
Rhodes 87
Boat to Haifa 95
Kibbutz 99
Jerusalem 103
Rotterdam 107
Epilogue 111

Paris

The boat pulled into the dock at Le Havre. Bicycling along the *quai* was a French policeman, cape flowing, jaunty *kepi* square on his head. He must have been paid by the Tourist Office to ride around the harbor. The trains waiting on the tracks were small, indicating the scale of space in Europe. I was dizzy with the anticipation of the next few months in Europe. We disembarked.

On the boat train into Paris I was anonymous, not deigning to communicate with the two American college girls in my compartment. La Seine, green grass, apple trees with black and white cows underneath, and small cottages looked ready for a picture in a French textbook. Three hours later it was too dark to watch and we pulled into the Gare St. Lazare.

Scrambling through the station to the street outside, I was intent on managing well. A small, gruffly man asked me, *"Voiture?"* Translated to "car" I ac-

cepted. We rode a few minutes to the hotel and he said thirty francs. Impossible that the ride should cost six dollars. He rattled in French and started to drive away with my baggage. I frantically reached for a notebook and pencil to take his license number. The concièrge came out to arbitrate. My mistake was that *voiture* is not a taxi, but a limousine. We settled on fifteen francs; I hoped that this fracas was not a portent of life to come.

Upstairs the room was garish. Curtains, bedspread, tablecloth were each made from a different bright red printed material. The washroom behind the little screen held the joked-about bidet. I relaxed on the soft bed and tried to find a spot for my head on the long roll of a pillow. In spite of the raucous colors demanding attention, I fell asleep.

Seduction by Paris begins the next day. To walk in her streets is to be made love to. In the neighborhood of the hotel on rue Boissy-d'Anglais, near the American Embassy, are many surprises. For some reason I do not expect to see cafés new and shiny with glass and chrome. Wooden tables and checked tablecloths were my movie image of Paris. Each side of the street is filled with fancy dress shops, boutiques with stunningly decorated windows, *parfumeries* exposing all the secrets of French cosmetics. Each restaurant exhibits a menu to savor. How could I take it all in?

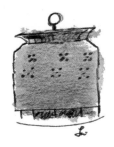

Walking to the Place de la Concorde I see the hag who sits and sells the lovely bouquets of flowers, each arranged as if for a girl to carry. The funny little cars maneuver without any apparent system around the Place. Again the scale of space is non-American. I feel large compared to the men and women in the street.

In the quiet of the Tuileries, shielded from the rush of the city by magnificent chestnut trees, women sit knitting while their young charges scamper in the gravel. Some of the boys earnestly sail their boats across the pond, plotting the course to the other side. The fountains are ringed with chairs. I marvel at the trustfulness of leaving garden chairs available. The air has a brownish cast from the trees. The sweeper, in *bleus* and beret, swishes his stickbroom, gathering the gold and rust leaves. No technological advances invade the park.

Notre Dame pulls me to the center of Paris. Looking up to the famous stained-glass windows, I begin to understand their fame. The rich colors flow around me. In my head I hear the great church music of the Renaissance filling the high vaults of the cathedral. So this is it.

During the day of walking, the contrast of the small intimate streets and the grand boulevards makes a dramatic event at every corner. The cars seem out of place, rather than the people as in America. The French women look absurdly feminine,

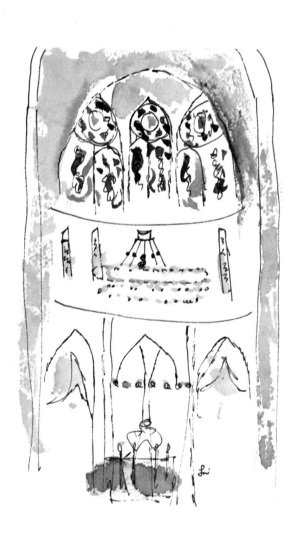

seemingly unnoticed by the blasé French men. The children are in tow, containing themselves on their little spindly legs. I float through the city in a first-day hypnotic state.

Dinner is early in the evening, as I am not yet accustomed to the French schedule. I choose "Le Frigate," on the Quai d'Orléans. It looks warm, inviting, and empty. The snippy waitress hands me *la carte* while I notice her faint smile. The menu-French I had acquired only covers the basic ingredients for a meal. "Cervelle de Veau" I read, recognizing of course that *veau* is veal and a safe choice. A small carafe of wine and a salad I manage to command without difficulty. The meat arrives: a lovely little calf's brain with butter and parsley! I am surely old enough to extend my palate. It is delicious. Paying the bill I feel like a seasoned traveler.

I make arrangements in a nearby hotel on the rue de Lille to move the following day from the right to the left bank.

Paris . . . it was all there.

Concièrge

Near the rue de Bac is a small hotel at 40 rue de Lille. It is pleasantly located one block away from the Seine and across from the Louvre. The *quartier* is old world elegance, with imposing buildings providing ample space for the carriages that once wheeled through the high doors into the cobbled courtyards. It is the neighborhood for antique furniture, careful restoration, and ancient curiosity shops. There is even a chamber of horrors selling antique medical equipment with illustrations. A few art galleries plunge this part of Paris into the twentieth century. M. and Mme. Achache offered a room for twelve francs a day. I installed myself by opening my two suitcases and spreading out several French dictionaries.

The narrow room had just enough space for the single bed. Again the flamboyant bedspread and curtains did not match. A tall *armoire*, or standing closet, was enough for my coat and clothes. The deep red carpet easily absorbed any water

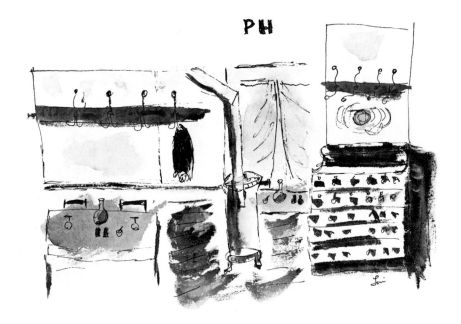

from my drip-dry system. The sink was functional, gurgling every time someone in the hotel used the plumbing. The bidet made a nice place for flowers. Along the bed were rows of shelves, convenient for all of my travel and French books. In this minimum *tout confort* there was a handy light switch near the bed and a telephone to call downstairs. Even the unfamiliar odor appealed to me.

Through the open windows was a continual view of Paris life. At the busy corner was a butcher shop. The butcher worked around the hanging carcasses of beef. He wore the traditional blue-checked outfit and always had a fresh apron. His apprentice swept sawdust, delivered packages from the wicker basket on his bicycle, and made himself helpful to customers during the rush time every evening.

On the opposite corner was a workman's café. The lady behind the counter was always cleaning it. On the counter was a little stand holding several boiled eggs and a salt shaker. The men leaned on it, gulping their *vin rouge* or *vin blanc* whenever they had a chance to drop in. A sign on the window advertised *"sandwichs chauds"* but I never saw anyone eat there.

If I leaned far enough out the window I could smell the bakery on the corner. The fragrance was most compelling early in the morning and in the afternoon, from the two fresh batches of

bread that were produced in the floury cellar. The simple rolls and loaves were a continual satisfaction.

The hotel had many systems that were new to me. Just beyond the small lobby with two huge, ugly leather chairs, and the crowded dining room, was the room of M. and Mme. Achache. They lived on the disheveled bed, watching television and reading the newspapers. The small kitchen was usually filled by the Spanish maid. The absurd *minuterie* lit the steep winding staircase only until you were out of reach of the next button to push to light it again. At the bottom of the stairs was a telephone with two earpieces and three volumes of the Paris telephone book, all cross-referenced by name, address, and occupation. Potentially the telephone system was practical, if you could hear when someone spoke. M. Achache kept a book for telephone charges and added fifty centimes each time the phone was used. On the second and fourth floors were w.c.'s.

Showering was a special system. I descended, asked Madame for the key and tried to take a shower in the quickly steam-filled closet. I learned that the best time for showering was between two and six in the morning, when the water was hot. The mysteries of the bath room were never enticing enough for me to explore. Considering all of these conveniences, I understood the heavy odors in the packed Métro cars on my rides to work.

Breakfast was a ritual. On teaching days I came downstairs to the dining room. It had an oilclothed table that seated four, usually someone's suitcases in the corner, a refrigerator, a chest of drawers that was also used as a desk, and walls filled with Madame's collection of gallery announcement posters, and four people. When I sat down, Madame would ask if I wanted coffee, tea, or hot chocolate. She would make up the order and bring back on an ugly printed metal tray the hot drink, a little glox of marmalade in a tiny dish, some foil-wrapped butter, a delicious roll, and a croissant from the bakery next door. Mondays, when the corner one was closed, we had to make do with an inferior bakery down the street. Following the example of the other guests, I split the roll lengthwise, buttered it and ate it with jam. Then I ate the croissant, trying not to sacrifice any of the crisp, delicious crumbs. Each morning the same breakfast was served and offered the same satisfaction. The guests changed often. We would try to make conversation in some common language. When I was alone, I would struggle through the newspaper *Le Monde* and Madame would explain words to me. On weekends when I stayed in town I ordered breakfast in my room. M. Achache would bring it, giggling about *café au lait au lit*.

M. and Mme. Achache performed all proper concièrge functions.

Madame told me where I might buy stockings, have my shoes repaired, which galleries were having exciting shows, and helped me make difficult telephone calls. They let me know who was waiting for me in the lobby and straight-facedly screened those people I avoided. M. Achache waited up for my return from a winter vacation on a Sunday night to give me a telegram that said school would be postponed for several days because the pipes were frozen in the old villa where we worked. Considerate of my modest teacher's salary, on out-of-town weekends they let me leave an extra suitcase in the dining room so that they could rent my room and not charge me for it. All year they struggled as they spoke French to me, enthusiastically correcting my mistakes. (One spring day I was coming down the stairs and heard some voices speaking English . . . some with French accents and some with Japanese. Apparently the Achaches would only speak their English under Oriental circumstances.) They were interested in reports of the many trips I made. When I left Madame warmly gave me some of her favorite posters from her collection. I knew I would see them again sometime.

Sion

I went to the American Embassy one day to find out if I needed a visa to travel in Yugoslavia. At the entrance I met Susan, a girlfriend from California who had just spent a year in Israel. She had been to the Embassy to see how she could find a job in Paris. We both decided right then that as soon as my car was delivered we would travel together for a month or so.

Several days later we waited for the new car at the factory showroom. Finally, at six in the evening, they handed me the keys and wished us *bon voyage*. Susan and I threw our bags into the trunk. I tried to drive through the evening rush traffic, remembering that there is only one rule of the road: the car on the right has the right of way. Susan read the crucial information from the owner's manual. The headlights needed adjusting and every on-coming car cursed at us. We found the national highway that leads south and headed for Switzerland.

Switzerland looks exactly like the calendar photographs. It is geographically dramatic, green, flowered, and full of peasants leading carefully brushed cows in front of chalets. The cowbells ring through the valleys. Every detail is perfect. The visitor has no doubt that this set is created for him.

Seeing a castle in the town of Sion, we feel compelled to explore. We park in the empty lot and I start the quick climb up a rock path. On the opposite side of the hill, Susan is exploring a small stone church, and we wave.

Hiking up out of the twentieth century, I feel the warm September sun on my back, and am dazzled by the bird reflectors on the surrounding fruit trees. The cartwide path leads to the castle walls. Across the gravel courtyard stands a small castle with gardens on each side. The top of the hill is level to accommodate the gardens and buildings. I gingerly step into what must have been a chapel. In the cool, stone interior there is still a painted design of flowers on the crude plaster. A medieval lady with her entourage brushes me as she wafts up to the altar. Climbing up to the back garden planted with rows of fruit trees, I hear the rustle of her silks. The castle seems to be lived in.

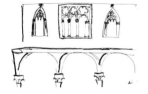

But it is not a delicate maiden rustling, it is a substantial brown goat, enjoying tender green leaves. I hold some leaves out for him and he leads me on

around the edge of the garden. I look down
the sheer cliff to the village below. The
brown goat leans out over the edge and
reaches for another soft mouthful. I follow
his eating tour down the path. Off to one
side is a small stone hut set into the stone
wall surrounding the castle. An old man
comes out. The goat trots up to him.

While the goat butts and
nudges at the man, we say *Bonjour*. He
joins me on the path and points up to the
openings in the stone over the castle gates.
This was the best location in the whole
valley. Hot oil used to be poured onto the
enemy through the openings in the wall,
he explains in slow Swiss French. How
lovely the castle is, how surprising to find
the walls still painted. He walks down the
hill, patting the goat at his side. He lives in
the stone hut and is concierge to the phan-
toms in the castle.

I see Susan waiting for
me in the car. Abruptly the castle people
vanish. The goat man wishes us a pleasant
journey, and we drive off in the brilliant
Swiss valley.

Gard

Susan and I started out one morning in the Renault heading for Aix-en-Provence. Marking the places of interest on our map we especially noted the one-star restaurant we would reach at lunchtime in Uzez.

Road signs advertised a museum of prehistoric artifacts in Les Matelles. It was difficult to find on the map but not far out of the way so we stopped in the small town. Walking through a narrow street we saw a handwritten sign, explaining that to see the museum, please ring the bell across the street. A frowzled woman answered the door and went to get the key to the museum. We walked around the dusty room, gazing into glass cases. There were stone tools, and shaped bones almost crumbling. We saw a leg bone with an arrowhead lodged in it. Provence had been peopled longer than we could guess. We each gave the lady a couple of francs and left.

The drive through La Garigue was filled with smells of lavender and drying hay. It is an area similar to the California chaparral. Bare, rock mountains, withered trees, a dried-up creek bed, sandy soil for vineyards were familiar to us. The sun was warm and the air was soft. We crossed a bridge and looked down to see women washing sheets in the stream. They put them out to dry on the rocks, with a river-tumbled stone holding each corner down. With the fresh running water and the sun's rays the sheets were probably as clean as from any "modern" laundry.

Susan and I enjoyed our lunch in the mountain town of Uzez. The restaurant was simple and decorated like a farmhouse. We relaxed on the wooden benches and plumped pillows as we drank local wine and ate stewed rabbit. The Provençal tomatoes and garlic sauce were intoxicating.

Friends in California had given me the name of a family living in Gard. While we were driving down the mountains from Uzez to the coast a truck passed with " Gard " printed on the bumper. We thought we must be close to that department in France when we saw several other trucks marked the same. At the first gas station we found out their town was only twenty minutes away.

We drove around the small square. The usual platin trees, or sycamore, shaded the whole square. Some old men in their *bleus* sat on the benches and talked. A group of skinny-legged boys played *boule*. Down one of the four streets leading away from the square we found the Le Conte house. The farm-sized courtyard was roomy enough for several tractors to park on the gravel. The ground level of the building was filled with farm tools and a chicken coop. We chose one of the stairways and knocked at the front door. Dogs yelped, chickens cackled, and a woman with children screaming behind her opened another door. The master and the family would be back later in the afternoon.

We took the opportunity of their absence to explore the beautiful grounds. Just beyond the house, a garden supplied tomatoes, green beans, onions, cucumbers, and garlic for the kitchen. The dahlias grew close together, to be used in the house. The path led past park benches through old trees, surely designed by the grandfather. The shade was a welcome change to the Mediterranean sun. Considering the scarcity of local w.c.'s, we took advantage of the privacy of the garden.

On our way back to the driveway we noticed a car parked in front of the house. We knocked again at the door and Madame answered. Over the noises of the hunting hounds echoing in the tiled hallway, I gave the name of our mutual friends in California and we were invited inside. The Le Contes were busy in the afternoon, but would we please come back in the evening for dinner. If we came early enough, we could help pick the *haricots verts*. All arranged, we decided to spend the afternoon in Nîmes.

By the time we returned in the evening the beans had been picked, but M. Le Conte invited us to walk with him to the creamery to pick up the ice cream that he had ordered. On the way he showed us the beautiful garden. As we strolled along the path he told us that his father had started importing these trees before the turn of the century. We remarked at the sturdy and plentiful bamboo, quite familiar to us.

We opened the jingling door of the creamery. Inside it was cool and sweet smelling. The colorful boxes of centime candy would tempt any youngster. On trays on the counter stood fanciful patisseries, heaped with whipped cream. The creamery lady took out of the freezer a small bucket of ice cream and packed it in a Styrofoam box. We walked quickly back to the house carrying it and some special cookies.

The house was older than the Revolution, when it had been remodeled to include secret passageways. In the dark, wood-paneled game room was a ping pong table. A stand near a window held an open Bible, hand printed on parchment in the 1700s. Upstairs were many small bedrooms. Each one had a four-poster bed, a dresser, and a lamp. The curtains, bedspread, and lampshade were decorated with local Provençal material in designs of red, green, and yellow. The parlor downstairs was arranged for conversation, with small groups of stiff-backed chairs. M. Le Conte led us to the kitchen where Madame and two maids were fixing dinner. All along the white and blue walls were pots and pans and unidentifiable cooking implements. In the sink was a hand water pump. The large wooden table in the center was heaped with fresh vegetables. The dogs' noses could just reach the edge of the table.

Susan and I were invited to sit down in the dark dining room. A low hanging lamp barely illuminated the wooden buffets around the tiled room. The table was set with a cloth that smelled of the sun. Our conversation about current affairs reminded us *when* we were.

Dinner began with eggs mimosa, fluffed hard-boiled eggs with freshly-made mayonnaise. Then we were delighted with a roast of lamb and the garden beans followed by a summer salad. The simple, fresh, superb food was the height of French cooking. Our ice cream was accompanied by fried, crisp, *oreillettes*. During the meal Madame was the perfect hostess. When her husband introduced a subject she embellished and elaborated the story, but never brought up a new topic.

They intended for us to spend the night, but as they had mentioned that they were leaving for a vacation in Nice the next day, we excused ourselves. The drive home to our hotel was long enough to savor the conversation and confections of our hosts.

Castelnou

In the foothills of the Py-
rénées is a walled town built on cliffs. It
has gathered a small population of artisans
and craftsmen who live and work in the
medieval stone buildings. A hollowed-out
cellar serves as an olive wood carving shop.
In another building a woman displays her
rough wool weaving. Two or three display
windows along the cobbled road have ce-
ramics in them. Embroidered fabrics, terra
cotta casseroles, guitars, and candles are all
made right there.

Since no cars are able to
get through the town gate or streets, Susan
and I had parked our car across the main
road and meandered through this tourist
heaven. A friend in Montpelier had given
us the name of the best of the simple restaurants. The owner was also the mayor of
the town. When we arrived at lunchtime
we brought greetings. The mayor seated us
at the table in the middle of the small cave-
like room. On the white plastered walls
were leafy, dried branches and some of the

local ceramic work. A fireplace was black from big logs. The dark tile floor kept everything cool. We ordered the *spécialités du pays*. Our lunch began with snails cooked in a wine sauce in a small casserole. We plucked them out of the sauce and their shells with a three-inch thorn. The main dish was rabbit stewed in another dark wine sauce. The country bread absorbed every bit of the sauce.

During our slurpings of good wine more people filled the room. One family filled the largest table with children, aunts, uncles, parents, and grandmothers. An older couple took the table nearest us. They pulled their chairs forward and rubbed their hands while they waited to feast. A young local foursome took a table near the door. Because of the plaster and tile surfaces everyone could hear what everyone was saying. Unlike many city places, the conversation became general. The temperature increased. The warm air was stirred by the proprietor racing from the kitchen balancing the bubbling casseroles. A young man came in to sing and play his guitar, as he does when the restaurant is crowded and his sculpture shop is not. The older couple offered us a cigar and we gave them some cigarettes in exchange. The whole crowd laughed as the two of us puffed. After three hours of eating and drinking, we maneuvered our way out and down the hill.

We couldn't resist the vine-covered garden displaying plates and bowls and tiles painted with whimsical, delicate flowers. I chose some tiles and Susan picked out a candlestick. The ceramist, an old man with a soft beard and voice, didn't know what the rate of exchange was on our traveler's checks but accepted our calculations. He invited us in to see his studio. The low-ceilinged room was spattered with clay. He had tiles and bowls stacked everywhere. A plank table held brushes and bottles of glaze. The country feeling was a contrast to the commercial shops we knew in the large towns.

By the time we emerged from the studio, the sky over the mountains had become black with clouds. True to its promise, a resounding thunderstorm broke all around us. We kept pace with the rain water running down the medieval streets.

As we drove down from the mountains the rain stopped. The sun made the wet fields steam. Alongside the road were families foraging in the tall grass, picking things up and putting them in baskets. When we stopped to find out what it was, a woman told us that after it rains the snails come out. They are collected and left to wander around inside a box for two weeks. By then they are rid of their impurities and are ready to be cooked in a stew. The old peasant dishes and the new folksy art had combined several centuries for us.

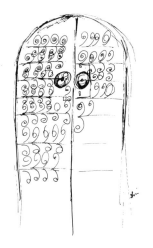

Arvika

In two months of traveling Susan and I had gone all over Europe and Morocco. Now we wanted to see Scandinavia.

After the long drive to Sweden it was pleasant to see the welltended fields. Each town gave us a feeling of order and comfort. The land looked like Minnesota, which is probably why Swedish people settled there. Everyone looked healthy and well-dressed. We noticed that many women worked in banks where we went to change money. But from the pleasant insides of houses we could see from the sidewalks, it didn't look as if their emancipation had ruined their homemaking interests.

We found the house in the suburbs of Stockholm that belonged to the family of a friend of Susan's. We languished in their hospitality for a few days. Each of the five family members has his own room. There is a spacious living room looking out to the garden. The dining room and kitchen are always warm and smell of baking bread. Each night at about eleven o'clock we join them in the Swedish custom of having something hot to drink and a light snack of bread and butter, cheese, herring, and cake.

Susan and her Swedish friend have a friend from their Israeli kibbutz who had accepted a teaching job in the town of Arvika, a few miles from the Norwegian border. We decide that it is a good opportunity to see him.

Again we hop into the Renault and drive through beautiful northern fields. The farmers are burning the hay that has molded from early rains. On the northern slopes of the fields skimpy patches of snow are starting the winter.

We get to Arvika about dinnertime and go immediately to the house in which the teacher rents a room. The landlady lets us in, telling us that he had left a week before, did not take any of his belongings, and has not left word. We wait in his room for awhile, reading his books.

Late in the evening, we walk over to see one of his colleagues. The wooden house is well-lighted inside. We can only get in with difficulty as the entrance is blocked by the collection of wool scarves, coats, and boots. The small living room has a hooked rug and a rocking chair, looking very much like an American farmhouse. We try to find an explanation but his fellow teacher is as puzzled as we are.

The next possibility is to spend the night in Arvika and see if there is any news in the morning post.

At the two moderately priced hotels the three of us cannot get rooms. It is Saturday night and many people come into town for the weekend. With our combined finances we can afford one room at the expensive hotel. The lobby makes us already imagine the hot shower and big beds waiting upstairs, but it, too, is full. We sit down in the main dining room and order beer. A small orchestra is playing dance music from the 1930s in America, and the women are dressed in corresponding fashion. Our tacky appearance must be disturbing to the local ideas of elegance.

It is getting late. We eliminate the possibility of sleeping in the small cold car. Our waiter suggests that we ask at the police station for someone who might rent a room for the night. About two o'clock the dining room closes. We head for the police station, punchy from the long drive, the waiting, and the beer.

We enter the police station and tell the officer our circumstances. He does not know of any room for the night, but leaning over the smooth counter he asks cautiously, would we mind sleeping in the jail? We look at each other and our Swedish friend replies in English that we would appreciate that very much if it is not too much trouble. With a straight face he tells the officer that he is John Smith from New Jersey.

Quite serious, too, the officer shows him to one cell, and Susan and me to another. The plain beds with clean sheets look good to us. Our unsuppressed laughter echoes down the jail corridor and the annoyed officer comes to lock the door. We will be awakened at seven in the morning.

Promptly at seven there is a sharp knock. We offer to pay for our stay, but the officer does not accept. Meeting our friend in the waiting room we avoid his twinkling eyes that would cause another explosion of laughter. We comment on how much more comfortable the jail is than some youth hostels we know. We go to the only café that is open to have an enormous cup of café au lait and wait for the English teacher.

Later in the morning we check again with the landlady. She has received a letter saying our friend has gone to England to see his girlfriend and could not stand to come back to the isolated town of Arvika. We take his things to mail to him and start the drive back to Stockholm.

Fontainebleau

Settled in Paris, teaching at the American School, travel was more local. As on many Sunday mornings, Jean-Paul, a family friend of one of my students, came to pick me up at my hotel in Paris at about seven o'clock one Sunday to hike in the forests of Fontainebleau. We drove to the Gare de L'Est in his tiny Citroën. That early it was not difficult to find a parking place. We went to the station café to have breakfast and wait for his friends who were going with us.

The café was warm and many other people were also up early. We ordered café au lait and each took two croissants from the basket on our table. Some other people tramped in with heavy boots and knapsacks, looking more like a climbing expedition than Sunday hikers.

Jean-Paul's friends joined us for coffee and then we all went to buy tickets and got on the train. We planned to take one train to the middle of the forest, and hike all day to another train station to take the ride back to Paris.

After a half-hour ride we were in wild country. The air was cold but pleasant, and the few clouds promised only a little rain. We started out, following a good map, through the rough terrain. During our hike we passed through meadows, granite mountains, sandy deserts, and dense forest. At each intersection of the well-marked paths Jean-Paul and his friend Phillippe argued about the right direction. By midmorning we found the cliff that the men practiced climbing. Each one took turns managing the ropes and yelling where the handholds were.

At lunchtime we arrived at one of the many huts in the forest that serve hot soup and coffee for hikers. It was crowded inside and it was beginning to rain. We looked around the back and found a woodshed where we set up our lunch. Each of us pulled out the food we had brought. Jean-Paul offered everyone his bottle of red wine, I passed around pieces of broiled chicken that I had bought the night before in a *charcuterie*. Phillippe lit his camp stove to fry a steak while we made fun of his extensive cooking arrangements. The rain at the edge of the woodshed poured down. By the time we were ready for coffee that was room for us inside.

The rain stopped and we continued our march, not any less briskly for having eaten a big lunch. Late in the afternoon we found the train station, a small building with a waiting room. We knocked on the office door to buy tickets but no one was there. Frantic, we looked around and saw the stationmaster on the other side of the tracks. He stood very straight with his cap on the back of his head and held a red flag high. Behind him stood another group of hikers. We pounded on the locked door leading across the tracks but he stood still. An express train clicked past. The stationmaster waved the flag and led the other group across the tracks into the waiting room. Very deliberately he opened his office and sold tickets just in time for us to catch the train to Paris.

We slumped into the seats and relaxed. At the Gare de L'Est we all said our good-byes until the next Sunday outing. Jean-Paul invited me to his place to clean up and enjoy a Spanish style dinner of meat and pimento. He drove me back to my hotel where I made preparation for the next day's work.

La Grande Chaumière

Near Boulevard Montparnasse and Boulevard Raspail is one of the oldest art schools in Paris, La Grande Chaumière, on the street of the same name. The enamel plaque outside proclaims in flowery turn-of-the-century gold script the names of the masters who give courses. In the evenings, drawing sessions with a model are presented without instruction and anyone can sit in.

Jean-Paul goes once a week to work from the models and invited me to join him one evening. We meet at a crowded, steamy café across from the Alliance Française. All of the students from the school are babbling in their own language . . . Spanish, German, Persian, Swahili. There is cross-cultural exchange in French. The one waiter tries to walk through to get the tiny cups of black coffee to the tables. Pale students are gulping pale, bready sandwiches. Someone wipes the condensed steam off the cold window to see if a friend is arriving. A little before seven o'clock the café starts emptying and we wrap into our neck scarves and walk the few blocks to the art school.

We pass through the narrow door and down the cold, dark, dirty corridor, our elbows brushing each wall. A man standing at the entrance to the studio takes our three francs. He is wearing an overcoat that long ago lost its shape, a woolen scarf wrapped around his probably scrawny neck, and is in great need of a barber.

Jean-Paul and I enter the small theater-studio from the back. The stage with one light bulb hanging over it is surrounded by tiers of drawing stools. The room is crowded with young men. They are all dressed as if for the wintry outdoors, with only their fingers and eyes exposed. Every available seat and step is filled. Not a word is spoken. The quick rubbing of charcoal and paper ripped from drawing pads are the only sounds. We perch on the back cabinets and begin to work.

On the wooden platform a model lounges on a dirty, upholstered chaise. She cuddles a thin cat which adds to the warmth from a portable electric heater. Her legs are red from the cold and the deep shadows under her eyes are accentuated by the overhead light. Her body looks tired, sagging at the belly. Her hands are red. Her hair is dark, cut short and not coiffed in any French style.

We work quickly, trying to keep up with the first pose of half an hour, two poses of fifteen minutes each, three poses of five minutes each. We use sticks of charcoal on grainy paper. Jean-Paul offers me some whispered suggestions of how to proportion the head to the body, and how to indicate toes and fingers. My lack of skill is apparent but he is encouraging.

At the end of the poses the model reaches for her clothes and quickly dresses behind the small screen. We pack our charcoals and papers and join the crush to the outside. Everyone is chattering. "That last pose was the hardest." "When are they going to have a male model?" "I'm hungry." "Once a week is not enough." Jean-Paul and I admit that we are hungry too and he suggests a place he knows.

Around the corner on rue Notre Dame des Champs we find the little restaurant whose light and noise spill out onto the street. Pushing our way through the crowded tables and stools we sit with some other art students. The room is small. Each of the walls is tapestried with bulging lines of coats and scarves hanging from hooks all around. The noise is at yelling level and the waitress does the most. She sidesteps, carrying dishes above her head. She shoves a greasy, illegible, dittoed menu at us. Next time around we yell at her what we want, and demand some bread and a demi-carafe of red house wine. We dunk our bread in the wine hoping the food will come quickly. Eating our sardines, roast veal and *haricots verts,* and wedge of Camembert we are interrupted by demands from other tables for the mustard, the salt, or to hear a funny story. We are all laughing, yelling, pushing food into our mouths and sweating. Jean-Paul and I gulp our last glass of wine and yell for the waitress to come take our money. We write down on the paper place mat what we eaten, she adds up the prices with a service charge and we leave our francs. We slide out of the door into the cold night.

Walking home through the *quartier,* with the windows shuttered and no light, we are still warm from our dinner.

Lascaux

The caves of prehistoric paintings at Lascaux were high on my list of pilgrimages. With great alarm, the French government had discovered that a green moss was beginning to grow over the paintings. Rumors that the caves would be closed speeded up my plans to visit them.

It was the middle of winter and warnings of *ver glas,* a thin sheet of ice, were posted on every road. I planned to make the trip from Paris in one day and stay overnight in Montignac. The tenseness of extra care made driving arduous. Overloaded trucks slipped all over the icy road. Truckdrivers stopped oncoming trucks to ask about the road conditions and compare their efforts. By late evening I arrived at the town in the middle of France.

Montignac was arranged like many other French towns. An old railroad station dominated the central square. *Boulangeries, charcuteries,* and *crèmeries* were busy with late customers. The scraggly trees offered little softening to the harsh winter. The hotel on the square where I found a room was grandly constructed in the 1890s but had been poorly maintained.

After arranging my things in the comfortable room I went downstairs for a late dinner. The white tablecloths and bright lights decorated the dining room warmly. The waitress quickly brought a bowl of hot soup and announced what the rest of the dinner would be. The only other people eating were three very young French soldiers.

When she came back with the wine she said that the young men would like me to join them. Not at all sure of my French, it seemed impossible. She convinced me by setting a place at their table. Their scrawny faces were bursting with anticipation and pimples. They were delighted to know that I was American. What kind of things do you buy in a drugstore? What is a milkshake made of? Are there really cowboys in California? Not only did they want to know about America but when I told them I was living in Paris they wanted to know about that, too. We managed adequately in our combined English and French. But worn out from the language struggle and the long drive, I declined the invitation to join them at a café for an after-dinner coffee. The country freshness of the soldiers lasted until the next morning.

I wouldn't accept the word of the concierge that the caves were closed and drove out to the site. The moist ground steamed in the weak sunlight. An old dog sniffed and barked at the hut which had signs posted over the windows. A fence closed off the path that led to the caves. The sign said that the caves were being attacked by the *maladie verte* and would remain closed indefinitely. Determined to watch the newspapers for the first opportunity to visit, I started the drive back to Paris.

Tunis

Friends from college who had joined the Peace Corps were stationed in Tunis. A fellow teacher and I accepted their invitation to visit during the winter holidays. We flew from the coldest Paris winter in twenty years. In Tunis, in December, the bougainvillaea splashes over the high walls, the dates and oranges are ripe, and the air is gentle.

After a few days of local sightseeing, our hosts were eager to check on the progress of a rug that was being woven for them. We had seen long skeins of dyed wool reserved for weavers hanging in the marketplaces. We borrowed a jeep to drive to the new, small dwellings, sprawling outside of Tunis. Many Bedouin now live in this government housing. Across the sun-bright courtyard in a dark room a loom was set up. In the one foot of space between it and the wall sat the weaving woman.

The Bedouin woman smiled in greeting; her gold teeth gleamed in the shadows. Her hands moved among

CARTHAGE

the wool strands. Squatting behind the loom she was entirely covered by her dresses of printed material. Between her eyebrows and on her chin and on the backs of her hands were traditional blue tattoos. She nodded and displayed the half-finished rug.

The colors of the rug were earthy reds, yellows, and browns. The woman pointed to some signs at the corner of the rug, which were supposed to be my friend's initials, but since she didn't know the Roman alphabet, they were undecipherable. The heavy wool rug would be a fine addition to our friends' apartment.

To celebrate our appreciative inspection, we were invited to join the household for lunch. We crossed the open court to a small bedroom where a table was jammed in between two beds. The four of us sat down with the rug maker and two other men. On the oilcloth table was a round, flat bread, and an unlabeled bottle of wine. The small house and the wiry people made me feel overgrown.

Instead of using a bottle opener, the man of the house made a circle of a wound-up dish towel and held it against the wall. He thumped the bottom of the wine bottle against the rag until the cork popped out of the bottle. We drank a toast with the raw, rose-colored wine.

A young girl brought in a large platter of beans in a red, oily sauce. I was handed one of the four forks. It slipped from my hand and broke in two on the

47

hard-packed dirt floor. I was assured that it didn't matter; all of the men ate with bread in their fingers. The delicious bean mixture tasted of peppers, tomatoes, and rich olive oil.

When we were finished eating, I made a motion to rise. The woman called to one of the young girls. She led me across the courtyard to a tiny slit in the wall. Inside were the two footstands that direct the use of the "Arabic toilet," which the Arabs claim is Turkish.

The sun startled me as I crossed the court to rejoin the party and finish our coffee. Dopey from the cramped quarters and the heavy wine, we tried to show our thanks for the shared meal. In about two weeks the rug would be finished and our friends agreed to come for it.

Altamira

My curiosity about the prehistoric cave paintings had not yet been satisfied when my mother arrived to visit me in Paris in the spring. In the northern part of Spain, near the town of Laredo, is one of the greatest sites of cave art, Altamira. It would be worth the long drive.

The closer my mother and I got to Spain, the hotter and drier the air became. At Laredo we found a pleasant hotel on the beach. To refresh ourselves we take a walk in the town, late in the afternoon. On each side of the main street we see many people standing and talking. We hear music made by horns and drums. Around the curve a small band parades solemnly. All the men have on white shirts and slacks, a red sash, and a Basque beret. The people on the sides view the procession silently. We watch this unexplained bonanza.

The next morning when my mother and I arrive at the empty parking lot for the caves, it is very warm and quiet. A guide stands at the entrance. His baggy and wrinkled uniform testifies to many days of work. He doffs his cap and we follow him into the first chamber. He explains to us that the paintings are deep in the caves.

We see some rooms with scrapings in the shape of animals, often with charcoal drawings done over them. In the largest room are the intensely elegant animals in reds and red-browns. The sensitive paintings range from the delicate to the masculinely aggressive. It is difficult for us to express our awe and wonder. After an hour of clock time in which we have tried to imagine the years of man's time, we emerge.

The souvenir shop has posters, cards, slides, and books. My mother and I buy an outrageous number of slides, thinking that they will capture the paintings for us. Two ladies scurry, wrapping packages, saying that there are more caves further up the dirt road if we are willing to go alone.

We hike along the road cut into the hillside until we come to two men just emerging from the caves. One of them, wearing a khaki shirt with the front open and dusty pants tucked into heavy boots, offers to take us to scrapings he has just discovered. We agree as four young priests saunter up, their long tunics with the tiny buttons all the way down the front sweeping in the dust. They are laughing and exclaiming over the beauty of the site, the mountains, and the exquisite paintings. They know just enough English to be happy to converse with us. The cave discoverer leads us all into the entrance of the new caves.

The air is damp. The first chamber is spiked with stalactites and stalagmites. We follow along the path as the cave man points out scratchings of cumbersome animals. The faint charcoal drawings are difficult to discern from the rough wall. Further into the passage he lights a torch to show "his" wall. He talks very quickly and points out the shapes of more animals. We hike back to the entrance and daylight, my mother and the young priests giggling.

Nearby is a temporary shack where the cave workers keep records of their finds. We visit with another weather-handsomed man and see copies they have made of the scrapings. My mother and I decline an invitation to join the two gentlemen for coffee in the town.

After a leisurely lunch in Laredo, we walk along the quiet beach, trying to absorb the marvel of the cave paintings.

Belgrade

By the middle of the summer, I was eager to go to the music festival in Dubrovnik, Yugoslavia. A fellow teacher from the American School had moved with her journalist husband to Munich. I thought it would be easier to leave my car with her for the summer, as I would be sailing across the Mediterranean.

I drove to Munich to visit for a few days. With my friend's assurance that she would give it a run every week, I parked the car on the street. Then I began the trip to Yugoslavia.

It is a long train ride to Dubrovnik. One day's ride ends up in Belgrade, after which it is necessary to take a smaller train overnight to Sarajevo, and then another all-day ride to get down to the Dalmatian coast. I willingly start the trip.

When the train gets to Yugoslavia I see that most of the engines are printed with GIFT OF THE AMERI-CAN PEOPLE and have a symbol of a handshake. The people on the trains seemed unmindful of the crowded conditions, for it is vacation time and they too are heading for fun.

I get off the train in Belgrade. It is late afternoon and hot. I carry a small suitcase, a flight bag, and a heavy woolen coat I have lived in all winter in Paris. I debate: Is it worth carrying the coat around for the chance I might need it to sleep on when I go deck class on the boat to the Greek islands? I search the train station for someone to give the coat to, but who needs a winter coat in this heat? In the ladies' room is a woman mopping the floor, who looks sixty but is probably thirty years old. I push the coat at her, and in her confusion she accepts.

It is still a couple of hours before the train leaves for Sarajevo. I check my bags, cross the bridge over the river, and climb the hill to the center of town. All of the signs are written in both the Roman and the Cyrillic alphabets. The people on the street look healthy but poor. Men wear gray floppy suits, sport shirts, and Japanese-style rubber sandals. The women are wearing scuffed shoes, no stockings, shiny skirts, and blouses or sweaters. It is a poor attempt to look like the Parisians. Most of the men seem thin and wiry but the women look substantial.

In the middle of town the tables and chairs from the café seem to take up whole blocks. The waiters, wearing unstarched and unpressed white jackets, stay on their own sides of the potted hedges that determine which café gets paid. Many of the men are wearing shirts and ties with their suits. There are very few women. The lights come on and make the whole plaza bright.

I am hungry and go into a plain cafeteria across the street from the busiest café. The neon light is bright here too, showing the plain wooden tables and chairs, the bare walls, and the few men who are sitting and eating. It is clean and not unpleasant. At the counter I choose some Balkan yogurt in a small bottle, a light yellow roll, and one of the many unidentifiable stews from the pots. The food looks meager after almost a year of French cuisine. When I pick up the fork to eat I am surprised by its lightness and I can easily bend it. The food is good, the people are quiet. I sit and look out onto the street.

In the early evening light, made bright by the lights, I continue walking during my short stay. The shop windows are plain. I hear three boisterous fellows, joking and laughing, behind me. *"Vous n'avez pas peur?"* I turn around and smile at them. "No, I am not afraid." They are devastatingly handsome. Each of them is very tan, one with blue eyes. They wear cotton shirts, rolled up on their chests for coolness. Their slacks and rubber sandals seem typical of the area. "Amerikanski?" "Yes." We talk in French. They have never met an American. What is a young woman doing out by herself? I must come home with them to meet their mother. Take the train in the morning they insist. We go to the outdoor café in front of the railway station and have a tall beer. They want to know all about me, what is it like in America, a rich country where everyone has cars and a swimming pool? Again they insist that I must spend a few days in Belgrade and must stay with their families. My determination to get to Dubrovnik is finally clear. The most handsome one relents, and offers to get me a seat reservation on the train. He gives me the address of a friend of his who lives near Dubrovnik.

We walk to the crowded train platform as the crowded train pulls in. All three fellows push their way through to find my seat. Then they come to lead me through the bodies. With many good-byes and a kiss on the cheek from each, they wave me off. Two tired looking women are standing near my place. With sign language I make them understand that we can take turns on the seat for the night.

Train to Dubrovnik

The train pulls into Sa-
rajevo early in the morning. I shuffle into
the station. The station is new, with high
ceiling and glass walls. In the café I eat yogurt and a roll. The waitresses look like
peasants who have just put down their farm-
ing tools. I am eager to look around, but
fatigue interferes.

I begin searching for the
train to Dubrovnik. After much question-
ing and confusion, I see a little train that
looks like the ones used in the American
western movies. It has a tiny, coal-burning
engine perched on narrow gauge tracks.
Lining the insides of the small cars are
benches of wooden slats, highly polished
by many years of use. I hold out the ticket
reserving a seat and try to find someone to
tell me where to sit. Leaning against the
window is a young man in a uniform of
gray shirt and trousers and a gray cap
adorned with a red star. *"Une place?"* I
queried. He shrugs his shoulders and points
to an empty bench. Then he comes and sits

near me. He is not a conductor; he is a soldier on leave.

The benches fill. A handsome man, wife, and two daughters sit across from us. They inspect the whole car, talking excitedly. Next to us sits a young man who introduces himself as Bronko, and his new wife, a beauty with black hair and blue eyes who is a nurse. He is broad and handsome, and disheveled by the heat. She is young, but her hands and legs show rough aging already. Everyone is talking very animatedly and they slow down to try to talk to me in English or French.

The train puffs out and our all-day journey begins. Each time the train goes through a tunnel the vacationers rush around trying to close all the windows against the smoke and yell "Tooooonel." Each time we stop at a small station along the mountain, we get some refreshments. We hang out of the window to buy a paper cone full of apricots, or to grab a hunk of white Serbian cheese. Some people in the car stick out their hands with a water bottle, and someone on the platform goes to fill it. My soldier explains that perhaps the next time he will be on the platform and would fetch water for someone in the train. This gesture is repeated at almost every station and is acknowledged with a momentary nod of appreciation. The day and the talking and the eating continue.

In the evening, we arrive at the lovely port of Dubrovnik. Everyone is standing among his baggage, making sure it is all there. A tram comes down the street. It is quickly filled with noisy tourists. The sun is just going down and the air is cool and smells of the sea. The quiet water slaps against the stone wall after everyone is gone. There are no taxis, but the soldier seems to have everything planned as he picks up my bags. I follow him up the hill where he stops at a new, beautiful hotel and orders a room for me. I thank him profusely, eager to rest, but he suggests that I clean up quickly and we go for a walk. I find it hard to refuse after his many kindnesses, but after half an hour testimony to fatigue shows and we say good night.

The next morning he is waiting at the hotel entrance still wearing the unpressed gray uniform. He explains that he wants to show me the town. We go out to the street to wait for the tram. When it comes we get on the open car that is pulled by the main one. There are a few old women in peasant costume carrying bushel-sized baskets of tomatoes. After a ten-minute ride along the cliffs overlooking the sea the tram stops in front of the gate of the walled town.

On the drawbridge are several men selling woven wool bags. They stand, smoking. Through the walls, down the steps, and we are standing on the warm, polished white stones of the town. In front of us is a fountain made of the same smooth stones. The main street extends about two

blocks and ends at a Venetian palace and an arched café. We start down the main street with the early morning sun already hot. There are jewelers' shops one after another, each displaying filigree silverwork made during the quiet winter. We turn a corner and are in the square that is the market. Tables are set up on wooden sawhorses. Mounds of tomatoes and onions and green peppers are on each table. Melons share a corner with a table covered with local dolls and wooden carved pipes for the tourists. The stones are slippery with squished vegetables. The peasant women go to each table and squeeze fruits. We walk back through the streets, looking in each store. There is a picture of Tito hanging over all the canned goods and stacks of clothing.

At lunchtime we go into a busy cafeteria. I sit down and the soldier brings two plates heaped with fried sardines. He shows me how to eat them: Holding each one by the tail he takes the whole fish in a bite. We finish with *burik sir,* a heavy cheese pie surrounded by flaky crust.

The soldier explains that he had been on his way home to Titograd, but had decided while on the train, to stop at Dubrovnik. Now he must leave. He asks me to walk through the town and we stop at one of the jewelers. He offers me a pair of silver filigree earrings which I hesitatingly accept. I thank him again and again. We walk to the tram which will take him back to the train station.

Several days later there is a devastating earthquake in his part of the country. I never got an answer to the letter of thanks I sent.

Lokrum

I am lying in bed, listening to the voices, trucks, and carts on the way to the market. In Dubrovnik the street activities start at four or five in the morning, with everyone working furiously from then until noon. In the afternoon it is still and everyone is sleeping. The activity starts again about five in the afternoon when everyone finishes up work, has a late, leisurely dinner, and sits in cafés until midnight.

Dressed and walking down the steps from my room rented in a private house, I eye the fat, luscious tomatoes in the garden and choose the one that will be ready for me after dark. I am heading for the boat that ferries swimmers to Lokrum, a tiny island which can be reached by a twenty-minute ride from Dubrovnik.

Lokrum can be traversed in a fifteen-minute walk. A walk up stone steps under pine trees is cool. In the middle of the island on the hill is a beautiful old mansion that now houses a pleasant, quiet

café and a museum. The grounds are surrounded by fruit trees with pine-bordered
paths leading in every direction. Toward
the middle of the day the whole island
throbs with the buzzing of cigales. The part
of the island used for swimming has black,
flat rocks tumbling into the water; it is easy
to find the perfect slope on which to bake in
the sun.

At the dock I sit on a
stone wall and wait. Even though it is early
morning, the sun is very hot. I put my head
on my arms and feel the warmth on my
back, making me drowsy. Three babbling
women in worn shoes, frizzled hair, and
grizzled hands, stop in front of me. I nod
my head in greeting, not knowing "hello."
They talk among themselves, then look
closely at my face, theirs frowning. I smile
weakly. One of the women puts down her
marketing basket and puts her palm on my
forehead to see if I have a fever. I immediately brighten and try to explain that I am
not a Yugoslav even though I am wearing
native clothes, and that I feel perfectly fine.
We all laugh, their missing teeth not showing, and they continue into town.

The boat comes and we
who are waiting hop in for the short trip
on the Adriatic. The motorboat holds about
twelve people. The canvas canopy makes
shade only at midday. On the island I find
my favorite place on the rocks. I can hear
two Scotch couples chirping how clever
they have been in taking the train so that

they have more money to spend in Yugo-slavia, and how envious all of their friends will be when they come home browned. I lie in my Zagreb-manufactured bikini and look like part of the landscape.

Later in the afternoon I slip into the perfect water. It is very salty and therefore has little growth in it. It is cool and clear, ink blue, and spoils one for swimming anywhere else. I bob around in its gentleness.

A rowboat approaches with two young men, their brown backs bare. "Would you like to go for a ride?" they ask me first in French and then in English. They pull me into the boat and we introduce ourselves. As we row around the island they tell me that they are students from Belgrade. We stop in a cove I had seen from the cliffs above and swim a race to the scratchy rock in the center of the turbulent waters.

Our conversation is simple and direct. They are eager to tell of their annoyance with the Tito regime. Yugoslavia is such a poor country that she has to swallow this political situation to survive. I remark to them how empty the grocery stores are and that peoples' clothing seems of such poor quality. Yes, things are very difficult, but so much better than they had been. Now a man could wear a suit, if not leather shoes, and not worry about starving. The young people all have a chance to look hopefully to the future. What did it matter if Tito's picture hangs in every little shop? The boys had one request of me as an American: Would I send them some Levis from San Francisco? It is difficult for them to buy goods not produced in Yugoslavia. We agree to meet later in the evening at a café so that I can get their names and addresses.

We have a few more races and they row me back to my spot on the rocks. I thank them for the boat ride and snooze on the rocks.

Walking from the boat in Dubrovnik, I stop in a café to have the usual yogurt served in a glass bottle with a long spoon, and the roll of just the right sweetness. I walk leisurely back to my room, noticing again the fat tomato.

Trebenje

One morning during my stay in Dubrovnik I remember that among my notes is the address of the friend of the young man I had met in Belgrade. The map of the Dalmatian coast shows his town of Trebenje in the mountains that rise from the sea.

Across the walled city and wooden drawbridge and outside the city gates is the tiny bus office. The man behind the counter is sweating. I buy a ticket for the bus at two o'clock, which takes a half hour to reach Trebenje.

In the afternoon the local "Greyhound" (or Dalmatian!) bus begins to load. I squeeze in between a young woman with a wailing infant and an old peasant woman dressed in dirty black clothes, straddling her basket of tomatoes. It is getting hotter and hotter and the bus is not leaving on time. The gesticulating people and shuffling of packages indicate that more tickets have been sold than there are places to sit. Someone must get off and wait for the next bus. Everyone in the bus seems to endure the heat. Smiling and talking animatedly we all try to distract the wailing baby. Somehow the problem is resolved and the bus maneuvers out of the parking lot. We start a slow climb up from the sea, clinging to a narrow road that looks like a mere decoration on the stern cliffs. Off the edge are private villas and luxurious hotels. Bougainvillaea spills down to the beaches. On the left, almost scraping the side of the bus, is the rock cliff with a few weeds growing. The mountains are bare from the deforestation suffered many years ago to supply timber for Venetian ships. As we wind higher, the air gets cool and a thunderstorm breaks.

We labor into Trebenje under the deluge. Across from the bus stop is the shaded town square, where a market of fruits, vegetables, and handcrafts from Herzegovina is held every Saturday morning. More people are waiting for our bus in an office smaller than the one we had left. I manage to get out and go to the man at the desk and to show him the piece of paper with the name of "Mitchki." He speaks to me in Croatian and I say, *"No razumi,"* I don't understand. Then he tries German, and I try French. He shrugs, I shrug, and we both smile. The bus is leaving with its load of people returning home from the market.

I stride into the street, hoping to find someone else to ask for

Mitchki. The station man comes running after me, opening his large black umbrella. He is gaunt, with prominent cheek- and jawbones, and wearing the usual no-color shirt and pants, held on to him by a cinched belt. We walk down the main street toward an official looking building. He asks each person we pass where Mitchki is. No one is in the schoolhouse. We splash down an unpaved side street, asking all of the children who are hanging out of the windows waiting for the rain to stop if they have seen Mitchki, the teacher. More shrugs.

One of the streets leads us near the rushing river to a two-story wooden building, painted bright blue. The bus clerk beams at me and says, "Turkishe House?" I grin back and nod in agreement. He thrusts the huge umbrella into my hand and gestures for me to wait.

In a few minutes he comes running back, carrying a six-inch skeleton key. We walk up the wooden stairs and open the door to the first room. It is ornately decorated in the Turkish style, with cloth-covered benches around the walls, and intricately carved cabinets. The latticed windows face the noisy river. In one of the glass cases are several silk gowns, giving off waves of opulence from the bright pink and orange glimmer, dotted with delicate buttons. My host insists that I try them on. I circle the low, etched table, set with a brass coffee server and tiny cups, noticing the ornamented knives hung along the walls.

We walk down the grass matted hallway to the main room. It is larger and even more luxurious. Every inch of every wooden cabinet is carved and inlaid with mother of pearl. We sit down on the bench, and I take out my sketchbook to try to copy some of the designs. My host smiles at my appreciation for his treasures. Motioning for me to remain seated, he rushes away. I hear him thumping down the stairs, opening a refrigerator. He rushes back with a plateful of square Turkish candy. Chewing the oversweet delicacy I smile at the young man. We inhale the rain-freshened air that drifts in through the slats of the windows. I wonder at the pride and delight that the young Yugoslavian, and probably the villagers, take in this leftover from the many years of Turkish rule.

Rested and tranquil, I thank him and we leave, locking up the blue house. We saunter back to the bus station, looking at the mountains, and glancing back at the museum. The rain has stopped and the brilliant sun and the shouting children are out. We get back to the office in time for my friend to sell the last few tickets for the last bus back to Dubrovnik. As I get on the bus, I wonder where Mitchki is.

Zagreb-Athens

A devastating earthquake hit Skopje. Festival activities in Dubrovnik were canceled; the country was in mourning. All tourists were leaving to get out of the way. The day of my departure for Athens all planes were being used to help the victims of the earthquake. The travel office advised that it was best to wait at the airport. Tourists gathered early in the morning in Dubrovnik to wait for the bus that took us to the new airport. Hours of waiting. A harried ticket maker said to take the next incoming Italian plane to London, get off in Zagreb, and then take the train south again for Greece.

Late in the long afternoon when the plane lands, I get on for the short ride to Zagreb. From there I take a bus to the train station, and get a ticket for the Hellas Express which passes through on Track 3 at four thirty. The train station is scattered with people waiting. Many of the women wear bright, printed skirts. The young girls have long braids. The wiry-looking men all have on the gray, poor fitting suits and rubber sandals I had come to expect. Among all of the bundles these people carry are large baskets of tomatoes. Some of them look more Austrian than the people I had seen on the Dalmatian coast. There is a group of gypsies squatting on the pavement, as if they are used to long waits.

Two young boys ask me to watch their things while they go to get food for the train ride. When they return we notice that it is six o'clock and no train has passed. The earthquake has changed the train schedule, too. By chance, I look over at Track 1, and there is our train.

We clamber aboard, stuffing ourselves into the little space left among people, crates, luggage, baskets, and bicycles. Another long ride begins, but I am lucky to be invited to share the compartment of some students. As we leave the station, we pass other waiting trains from Eastern Europe, filled with people looking grayly out at us.

In our compartment we settle in for the long night. Accepting the offer of a top couchette I try to get comfortable on the hard, stiff bench, using my flight bag as a pillow. There is nothing to do but sleep; the train rolls too much for reading.

At dawn there is noise on the train of people scurrying, opening windows, and moving baggage. The train is passing through earthquake-ruined Skopje.

The buildings are cracked. People are sitting in heaps of cement rubble. The faces we see from the train are dazed and expressionless. The rumor passes from the next compartment that there are still people buried under the wrecked train station. I think of the young soldier who had been so gallant in Dubrovnik.

Later we are rushing through the dry mountains of northern Greece. The land that we see from the train is bare and rocky. Somehow the skinny sheep find enough to eat. Occasionally we pass a whitewashed hut with tobacco leaves drying alongside the house. While I am trying to get some air hanging out the window, a Negro from England who is on a teaching vacation, joins me in conversation. I notice that he, like other non-American Negroes, is confident of himself as a person. Greece looks so poor that it is hard to understand how the people have survived through the military occupations with their determination for freedom.

The dining car has been switched to an 1890 wooden club car, with Victorian lamps, dead in the sunlight. Perspiring in the 120 degrees heat, men in white shirts and slacks pant through the car, selling blackberries speared on sticks, and *soufliki,* Greek lamb and onions on sticks. The view I had seen early in the morning comes back: the rubble of Skopje. The geranium baskets were hanging askew at the train station.

Iraklion

At twilight, sitting at the busiest cafe on the island of Crete, I looked into the Mediterranean. The recurring fantasy of ancient boats slipped across my vision, this time they were light reed-sailed Egyptian boats. The ocean spray caught the bright lights from the café. I had been planning to come to Crete since I had read as a child about the discovery of Knossos.

Sharon, a New York social worker, whom I had met on the flying sewing machine from Athens, had accompanied me to the café. We sat listening to *bouzouki* music and watching the three dancers. Each of the two men had a great dagger thrust into the red sash that held up his billowing Turkish pants. The woman wore a long skirt, white blouse, and a red bolero over her full bosom. The *bouzouki* players twanged faster and faster while the three danced out the traditional triangle until one man won the girl.

After the performance all the people in the café danced. There were old men with their granddaughters, young lovers, old lovers, matronly wives with mustachioed husbands, young girls with even younger little brothers. The waiter served us honeydew melon in big chunks, which we ate off the tip of a knife, dribbling the luscious fruit into our mouths. We drank heavy, fruity wine, and became dazed by the lights and the music.

Two young handsome Greek Army officers asked Sharon and me to dance. George, on leave from Athens, told me that this was his hometown and that he was very happy to be able to show his family how good he looked. He spoke his English extra loud whenever we danced near someone he knew. Even though he loved the excitement of the big city, he was glad to be in the warmth of his island. Late, late in the evening we four left the café. In my wine-exuberance I walked along the narrow wall that separated the road from the water thirty feet below. In spite of everyone screaming at me not to sacrifice myself to the sea, I skipped along. The young officers escorted Sharon and me to our hotel. George proposed a visit the next day to the museum full of artifacts from the diggings at Knossos.

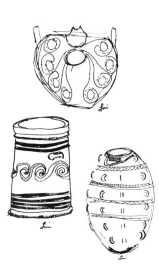

We met the following morning to walk through the town and to the museum. From our hotel up the hill from the harbor, we went to the main plaza. The fountain was surrounded by little boys, making pests of themselves by splashing each other. Since it was midmorning, the cafés were already filled with men sitting and drinking tiny cups of Oriental coffee. (Not called Turkish coffee in Greece!) Some old women in long black skirts and shawls passed by, bent, lugging string bags of vegetables. We followed some through the market. George said we would come back there for lunch.

At the museum we moved through the exquisite collection. Ceramic pots with wild, life-loving flower designs. Clay figures of the gods with arms raised. A golden bull. The diminutive but powerful snake goddess. Double life-size frescoes of bare-breasted dancing women, unfortunately and audaciously restored. Gold earrings, necklaces, cups. The double-edged sword, called a *labrys* in Greek and found in the winding tunnels that were given its name. George was proud of the display of elegant, joyful remnants.

Unable to contain more wonder, we went back to the market street for lunch. From each covered, open stall came smells of spices, stewing meat, sweet melons, grapes, peaches. The street was only a few steps wide, with a running gutter in the center. In one store there were huge square bins of dark brown, red, yellow, white, pink, and speckled beans. An-

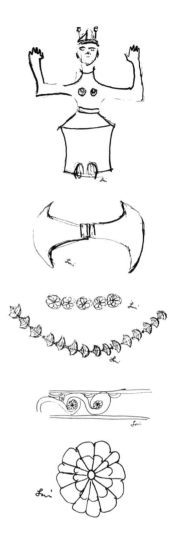

other had hanging carcasses of lamb and goat. Another had dried fruits and nuts. White fresh cheeses sat in their own thin liquid. Barrels of black olives made the street even more narrow.

On a small side alley was the street of restaurants. Each had small tables with handwashed white tablecloths in front. Each had a tiny kitchen which was completely taken up by huge pots of hot and cold stews. We walked up the street, looking into all the pots. George let me choose a table.

Following the local custom, after the waiter acknowledged us, we went to the kitchen and pointed to each pot we wanted to try. Eggplant and meat, tomatoes and olives, and other unidentifiable temptations we washed down with the local heavy red wine. Satisfied, we called to the fruit stand. A boy brought us a bunch of grapes. Our waiter brought a bowl of cold water for them to be dipped in. We sat, spitting seeds, watching the people go by. A couple of old men, obviously bowlegged in spite of the Turkish pants, were mumbling. I asked George why they chose to wear the Turkish outfit even though the Greeks hated the Turks and their long history of domination. He had no explanation. Some pale young women tripped by on high heels. George said it was very sad about them. Many had married American soldiers and had children, but the American soldiers went home without them. A Greek Ortho-

dox priest, with cylinder hat and hair pulled back at the neck, nodded good day to us. A group of little boys passed, each one eating pistachio nuts from a paper cone, and dropping the shells on the street. As the noon-time got hotter, the activity quieted down. The fat men were closing shop for the afternoon. I felt drowsy. We decided to meet in the evening to go to another café with music. I went back to the cool, tile-floored hotel for a nap.

Crete

Sharon and I have managed to find the bus that goes to the beach. A fifteen-minute ride takes us to the gate where we can see sun-browned natives lying on the sand. There are small groups of families and a few old women watching children playing in the surf. There is also a collection of pale, fleshy Americans from the Air Force base. We hike a short distance away from the lemonade stand with the umbrellas hatching more Air Force fellows down for a relaxing afternoon.

Behind us is the bare and awesome Mount Ida, where Zeus is supposed to have been reared in a cave. The waves of the Mediterranean are low and closely repetitive. The white sand is warm. I excuse myself to walk the whole length of the beach and cool my feet in the surf. Pink scallop shells chatter and scrunch in the water.

As I practice skipping stones, I notice a young, tanned man trying to outskip me and smiling devilishly. The whites of his lustrous Greek eyes and his teeth compete with the glare of the sun. He says, "Me Nikki. You?" I point to myself and say my name. He does a few skips around me. We continue together, walking up the beach. He draws a funny face in the sand with his big toe and writes his name under it in Roman letters. I make another face for my name. We laugh. The salty water drips from our hair and the waves knock gently around us.

When we get to the water-pocked rocks at the end of the beach, we sit down and look seriously at the sea. There are only us, the sun, the sand, and the movement of the water.

After some moments Nikki gestures to climb down the rocks. We stroll back to my spot on the beach. I introduce him to Sharon. We all lie still in the sand for a long time. When it is time to go, I quietly say good-bye to Nikki on the beach.

Rhodes

In Athens after a lovely week in Crete, I began finding out about how to get to the Greek island of Mikonos I had heard so much about. Small Greek boats take passengers to many of the islands. Since the trip is short and the weather mild, it is reasonable to go deck class. It is only necessary to appear at the harbor in Piraeus and find a boat going to the chosen island.

I left the YWCA and took the train ride to the port. Finding the agent for the boats to Mikonos I went to buy a ticket. Sorry, but all the boats are filled with people who have made reservations. Seeing my disappointment the agent suggested I take the boat that was leaving immediately for Rhodes. The inconvenience of going back to the hotel and starting all over again, or of hopping on the boat without any provisions for the two-day trip did not leave a clear choice. The boat horn blew and I ran to get on.

The top deck behind the smokestack was reserved for us lower-than-tourist class passengers. Each of us set our belongings on a spot near the railing that would be our table and bunk for the trip. Most of the people on the deck were young. There was an Italian couple with a Greek intruder who argued in triangular fashion all day and all night. By dawn the next morning, the Italian had gotten so outraged by the Greek's persistence and his girlfriend's lack of resistance, that he picked her up and threw her on the deck and went to find another spot for himself. A husky college football player from the United States was visiting grandparents he had never seen. Fortunately, his parents had taught him enough Greek so that the venture might be fun for him. Another man, somewhat older than the group, noticed that I was new to this method of travel. He showed me the best spot on the deck to avoid the wind and the soot. He was on vacation from his position of teaching German in a Greek school. He had left Austria in the late 1930s and had lived in India for over twenty years. We spent many trip hours discussing the differences of the civilizations.

When lunchtime arrived the others pulled out from their sacks fruit and cheese and wine and bread. Seeing me without provisions many of the group offered something of theirs. I didn't feel I could accept so early in the trip and went to buy a dish of spaghetti shared from the meal for the crew.

The day and the ship sailed on. Comfortable breezes kept the sun from making us too hot. Every few hours the boat stopped at a tiny, bare island. In a cove for a harbor, we would see blue fishing boats, and bright white and pastel stucco houses. The bareness was breathtaking. It was difficult to understand how these people survived without plants or crops. What did those goats on the hills eat? When it was dark in the evening, we could see that many of the islands had no electricity.

By the end of the next day the boat arrived at the substantial harbor of Rhodes that had been restored to medieval grandeur. I was glad that I had not dragged my heavy coat along. The pleasant beaches looked inviting. But they would have to wait for the next day.

After a few days of beach life, I am ready to change pace. On the far end of the island of Rhodes are excavations at Kamiras. The bus goes to that end of the island once in the early morning and returns late in the afternoon. It is a dramatic ride along the coast. I am the last passenger to get off in the desolate spot, where a barely open café overlooks the gentle sea. Near the café there is a little inlet with flat rocks, warming in the hot morning sun.

I start walking up the narrow road through the olive trees. A huge tourist bus with a group of Swedish people overflowing the island grinds to a stop for me. At the excavation site, my archaeologi-

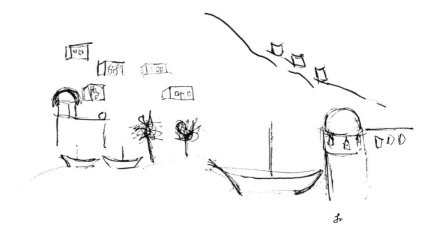

cally uneducated eyes cannot play imaginatively enough with the ruins. The steep hill covered with paths and loose stones does not signify anything to me. I half run down the sides of the hill, trying not to listen to the droning voice of the guide.

It is still early and much too hot to spend the day on the rocks waiting for the bus. I put my beach towel over my head for protection from the sun and start along the road leading back to Rhodes and the beach where umbrellas are rented. It is very quiet. I hear waves breaking mildly on the rocks, insects busy before the real heat of the day, and my sandaled feet slapping along the pavement.

Putt, putt, putt. A Lambretta pulls up beside me with a smiling Greek young man and a large box on the back. "Rhodos?" I ask. "Rhodos!" With his nod of assent and invitation to straddle the the box, we start off.

We slow down and stop. He walks into the fields to urinate. We continue for a few minutes and stop again, this time at the edge of a fig orchard. The young man picks some fat, green figs and shows me how to eat them. He holds one in his hand, and peels the skin from the blossom end to the stem, and then savors the whole fig in his mouth. We again continue on the Lambretta.

A few more minutes along the road and we are in the middle of a vineyard. We jump into the fields and break off several clusters of dusty warm, black grapes.

As I put a bunch into my mouth, the Greek admonishes me. We continue to drive on for about half a mile. We pull up at an unpainted café, which takes as little space as possible from the orchard. The wooden tables and chairs, sitting on the slab of cement, are well worn. Two grizzled old men sit with coffee cups. We sit down and in a moment the waiter appears with a large bowl filled with cool water, into which we dump our luscious grapes. We eat them all, trying to make conversation by gestures, but it is ludicrous.

Refreshed, we start again. We turn inland onto a small dirt road. "Rhodos!" I accept his confirmation. Perhaps there is an inland road to the town. We climb the hill. I cling more tightly to his waist as we skid over the gravel. At the crest of the hill, he stops again, pointing to the Lambretta and indicating that the motor is too hot. He tries to take my hand to lead me to the side of the road to sit under a tree. But I have spied a pear orchard. Weeds under the small, young trees are dry and brittle and the sun beating down on them makes them give off a yellow hay odor. I inhale deeply. I bring some pears to the resting driver. Again, we try to make conversation and give up. He finally resorts to making a universal gesture with his fingers and says, "American girls, yes?" I pretend that I don't understand and ignore his persistence. Finally, I get annoyed enough to start walking determinedly down the road, heading for the coast. He comes running after me, asking me to please get back on the scooter. He seems innocuous enough so I get on the box on the scooter.

We slowly wind down the road. I catch a glimpse of the sea over his shoulder. We bounce across a paved road and stop in the back of a restaurant. A large, dark woman comes out of the doorway, wiping her hands on her apron, and smiling a gape-toothed grin. "Mamma," the Greek fellow calls. They unload the box I have been sitting on. They bring it into the kitchen and introduce me to cousins, aunts, brothers, and open the box full of fish.

They immediately start scaling the fish. I accept the cold beer and a chair under the reed awning in the front of the beach restaurant. It is still early and all of the oilcloth-covered tables are empty. The Greek comes out, offering me some coins and pointing to a bus in the parking lot. "Rhodos." I try to thank him and explain that I have enough money. I run to catch the bus.

The bus stops several times to pick up young girls with baskets, who sit near the driver and giggle in exchange for their fare. When we get back to the town of Rhodos, I find an umbrella to rent on the beach and sit down to watch the locals, the tourists, and the sea.

Boat to Haifa

Israel: The furthest point in my journey, half way around the world. I was eager to see this country of contrasts. I was interested in the economically necessitated living arrangements. I wanted to know what Israel would mean to me. I had heard many stories about how innovative, exciting, and sometimes disappointing, life was there. My friend Susan had told me, on our long drives across Europe, of her life there the year before. She had lived on an *ulpan* to learn the language, and had worked in Tel Aviv. In the range from the agrarian to the urban, where might I fit in? I wanted to see the desert, to taste the Arab food, to see what this new country was like. A friend of mine from college had been living there for several years with his wife and children. They assured me of a place to stay on their kibbutz and a chance to live the communal life.

The boat from Rhodes to Haifa was a fine Greek ship, the S. S. *Agamemnon*. The cabin assigned to me was

formerly that of Lady-in-Waiting to Madame "X." At the table in the dining room were a friendly American couple from Boston. A young man joined us, who had flown to Athens from Los Angeles a few days before and was still in culture shock. He remarked that he had not watched television for three days and was amazed that he didn't miss it. The other fellow at our table was a Greek dancer. During the school year he taught gymnastics at a high school in Cyprus. For the summer months he went on tour with a professional folk dance group from Athens. When our boat stopped at Nicosia, he returned to his school, his fiancée, and the many problems of his island.

During the heat of the second day, our boat entered the harbor at Haifa. The enormous crowds on the dock made me think that many celebrities were among us. The closer we got to the dock, the bigger and noisier the crowd became. People climbed up poles to wave. Everyone was yelling. It was a multitude of welcoming. We passengers felt as if we were the first boatload of immigrants. Some Israelis returning from vacation said that the greeting for every boat was just as enthusiastic. It was difficult not to get caught up in the excitement of reaching the Promised Land.

After debarking, I managed to push my way through the crowds of hugging, crying, shouting, kissing people to find a taxi. As we drove up the beautiful hills of Haifa I could still see the swarms of people around the boat. Susan's aunt, who lived on the top of Mount Carmel, was willing to have me stay overnight with her family so that I could go to the north of Israel the next day.

Her house was very plain, with a scanty garden. The tile floors made it seem cool. However, the noise of the five children was thereby increased. Susan's uncle was a big trucker for the *Histadrut,* the national labor union, and was busy working day and night. I declined his offer to wait to catch a truck going in my direction and took the earliest bus.

The sun was hot as I walked to the terminal in the main part of town. I sat down on the benches to wait with the others. Most everyone looked European: women with shopping bags, men in open shirts, but carrying briefcases, youngsters in shorts and sandals. The bus driver arrived and settled into his seat with his cashbox by his side. He wore no uniform and looked tired and grouchy. He grunted for us to get on. When I asked him if he would let me know where to get off to find the road for the kibbutz, he grunted again, apparently in affirmation. I sat right behind him so that I could catch any little signal he might part with.

After an hour of driving with the hot wind blowing through the open windows, he stopped the bus for me and pointed across some fields. I followed the narrow road and took the first path.

When I got to a cluster of houses, I asked a brown-eyed boy for Shimmon. He pointed to a small, shacklike building. It was the middle of the afternoon and very quiet. I knocked at the screen door. Shimmon, who had been "Stan" in America, yawned and opened the door with a friendly greeting.

Kibbutz

The kibbutz Neot Mordecai, near the Sea of Galilee, grows tart Granny Smith apples. It has been settled since the 1930s and is comfortably established among its fields and orchards. Shimmon, his wife, and I exchanged gossip about friends in California. After our rapid reacquaintance conversation, they showed me to a wooden shack that many summer visitors had used. It had a metal cot on the cement floor and a few shelves. Part of the bathroom facilities were a walk down the path. In the other direction there was a shower on a cement slab, wooden boards, and only cold water.

The kibbutz was laid out like a camp with the main dining room in the center. Every morning we could go there for tomatoes, cucumbers, bread, and yogurt. The main meal was at lunchtime. The Czech cooks managed to continue their delicious cuisine: pickles, stewed meats, applesauce, and baked vegetables. Supper was the same as breakfast with the addition of herring or cheese. At each meal we drank apple juice, as the water from the Jordan was not safe. The service was cafeteria-style. Everyone sat at tables of four or six, discussing the latest work problems or local gossip.

Around the dining room were the children's houses, the library, the café, and three-story apartment buildings. Further out toward the fields were the shoe factory, the apple-packing plant, the work office, barns, chicken coops, and vegetable gardens. Near the river was a recreation field and a movie screen on the communal lawn. The kibbutz members had plans for a swimming pool and flower garden.

Life was like camp, too. It was possible to talk to anyone and ask many questions about communal living. After three days of being a visitor everyone must work in order to stay on the kibbutz. Since it was high season, I joined the harvesting. Bubka, the supply sergeant, fitted me from the common store with a pair of shorts, a shirt, some boots, and a *kova tembol,* "idiot hat." Many of the other migrant workers were Danish students. A bond existed from World War II when the Danes had protected many Jews. Students found the kibbutz a cheap vacation and were welcomed for the picking season each summer.

Work began at four o'clock in the morning when we all met near the barn. The tractor pulled a cart that we jumped into and hauled us to the orchards. We were given a fifteen-foot aluminum ladder with one pole to throw into the tree for balance. Each of us strapped on a specially designed canvas basket, which opened from the bottom to let the apples tumble gently into carts that were hauled by tractor to the packing house. Picking apples, perched on a high ladder, our faces in the leaves, we couldn't see each other. But we could hear everyone's voice. The Danish students sang and asked me repeatedly to sing "Old Man River."

Our work was scheduled to avoid the heat. We picked until seven in the morning, when we all met under the trees at the field kitchen to have breakfast. Big bowls of cucumbers, onions, tomatoes were on the table. We cut them up on our plates and poured over them *leban,* loose yogurt. Stuffed and rested, we went out into the orchard again. At about ten thirty someone came around with a can of coffee and salty rolls. We worked again until noon, when a tractor came to haul us away. We took cold showers, went to the big dining room for the delicious Czechoslovakian-style dinner and then swam in the Jordan. After our supper we went to the kibbutz café for conversation and coffee. We were free until four o'clock the next morning.

Eric, the village idiot, fastened his attentions on me. In his late thirties, desperate to find a wife, each summer he tried again with the visitors. He bicycled to the shack where I slept to wake me early in the morning. He offered the use of two blankets, which I didn't need, but which he left on my bed one day. He followed me to the apple trees and told stories. At the morning break he brought me rolls and coffee and insisted that I have more than I wanted. Hidden in the apple trees, rejected by me over and over again, he started making obnoxious remarks. Several days later, in his position as leader of the apple pickers, he told me that I had been transferred to the packinghouse.

Working in the packinghouse was not as pleasant as being in the trees, but while I put cardboard lining into the wooden apple boxes, I had a chance to hear stories from residents of the kibbutz. One day when I returned from work the extra blankets were gone. I knew the attack was over. From then on I could enjoy the hard work and companionship of being in a small farm community.

Jerusalem

During the few weeks of apple picking I imagined what it would be like to live on the kibbutz. Could someone who came from the anonymity of the big city live in this small town intimacy? While I was thinking of whether to stay or to go I went to see the Chagall windows in Jerusalem.

The bus ride was long and laborious. At each half mile of the road there was a burned-out truck commemorating the war of 1948. Up at Jerusalem the city sprawled over the hills. The pace of the traffic increased. I transferred to a local bus to go to the Hadassah hospital, where the windows are, a few miles out of town. Some young boys got on the bus. They wore long wool black coats, knickers and black stockings, round hats and long curls over their ears. In spite of the heat they looked as pale and cold as mushrooms from a cellar. Their faces stared out from the Middle Ages in the Eastern European ghettos. Centuries divided them from the robust kibbutz children I had grown used to.

The bus followed around many hills. Around the curves of each hill were terraced paths and prickly pear cactus, left from the Arab dwellings.

At the hospital there is a small chapel surrounded by rose gardens and a lawn. On each of the four sides of the chapel are stained-glass windows done by Marc Chagall. The reds, yellows, greens and blues are deep and the figures are lively. They are a tribute to Man, unlike the majestic cathedral windows in Europe which are a tribute to a God. They are beautiful, pleasant, delightful, but not awe-inspiring. They are of the twentieth century, when we have mastery of our destiny, and do not need religious miracles.

I spent the rest of the day walking around the special city of Jerusalem. It was exciting to see the conglomeration of people using the same sidewalks. Arabs, Jews, Europeans, North Africans, Indians, Sabras. Monks, priests, rabbis, the devout of every religion. Healthy youngsters, bearded old men, round-backed women. It was a feast of peoples.

I stopped at a stand to have a *felafel,* the local version of the hamburger. A round Arab bread is split to form a pocket. Into this go little balls of fried chickpeas, sauerkraut, chopped onions and green peppers. Over this and filling all the crevices goes a white garlic-y sauce of *te-hina,* made from sesame seeds. The first bite begins a lifelong addiction.

I felt I had not yet had enough of Israel and went to the boat agent's office to change my tickets to a later reservation. Perhaps within two weeks I could decide how strong a pull the country had.

I followed Shimmon's directions to his uncle's apartment in the new part of town. When his aunt opened the door she was amazingly like many of the women I had seen on the sidewalks. Her dark hair was short. She wore a plain cotton sleeveless dress and no adornments. She looked free from European ideas of femininity. In meager English she explained that her husband was away for a few days. I was welcome to stay if I didn't mind that we couldn't converse. She showed me the couch I could sleep on. The living room was stacked with bookshelves and more books were piled on a large desk. She invited me to a simple supper of yogurt and vegetables at the kitchen table. I tried to ask her about life in Israel. She waved her hand, indicating the three-room apartment. "It is very good."

Next morning, over hot coffee, I thanked her and promised to bring regards to Shimmon. I was eager to get an early start back to the kibbutz.

Rotterdam

Two weeks was enough to give me time to think about staying in Israel or going back to California. How to live, where to live, what to live for? The kibbutz is too small. The cities are not big enough. Israel is far away and all alone in an uncomfortable political situation. California is a good place to live. I was ready to start home.

The road leading from the kibbutz to the main highway is lined with eucalyptus trees that had helped drain the land of the malarial swamps. I follow the road to meet the bus to Haifa. From there I take a boat to Greece, a train to Munich, and drive my car to Rotterdam. The car is loaded on a freight boat and I have several days until the *Statendam* sails for New York.

Through the VVV, or Dutch tourist office, I have rented a room in a private house. There is a small bed made up in the book-lined study. I join the family for breakfast of boiled eggs, hot rolls with chocolate sprinkles, and hot chocolate to drink. The daughter of the family practices her English with me each morning.

The day arrives for the final good-byes from the Continent. After I wake up it doesn't take long to dress, as I have been sleeping in my clothes against the cold. I pack my flight bag and carefully go down the steep Dutch stairs. Outside the day is gray and cold. I catch the trolley to the harbor. It is too early to board the ship, so I walk up and down the cobblestone wharves. Getting cold I go to the nearest café. The tables are covered with Persian rugs, and the air smells of good Dutch cigars.

After a cup of tea I return to the wharf to look at the ship for a long time. A blind accordionist moans a melancholy song. I keep giving him enough florins so that he can accompany my tears.

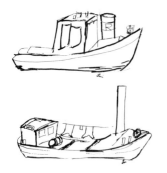

It is time to take the harbor boat through the busy water traffic to the embarking area. On board the ship, I am directed to my cabin. The luxury of an endless supply of hot showers and clean towels dispels my ambivalence. We passengers are invited to an enormous buffet. I begin to explore the tidy Dutch ship and my last European "home."

Epilogue

Many times during the months abroad I considered the possibility of remaining indefinitely. Daily life in Europe appealed to me: there were many opportunities for human contact. Cafés, small groups, a reasonable pace of activity, and short distances seemed to give people time to *be*. The follies and problems of America stood out sharply from that distance.

The American Schools all over Europe offer the chance to country hop: once employed by one school, it is possible to keep going from school to school. Rome, Moscow, Athens, Madrid offer tempting positions.

But in a journey there comes a time to go home, no matter how glorious the scenery, the people, the new experiences, the food and wine. The time had come for me. I had experienced the loss of reality that comes after continual moving. Struggling in French, or hearing some other foreign language, I began forgetting English! It became frustrating to be always absorbing and learning and not giving back. A need to create my own environment, a need to work grew in me and I felt I had to go back to teaching in a familiar setting.

A single young woman traveling in Europe can have lots of fun meeting new people and having adventures. But a single girl *living* in Europe is an anomaly. Europe is bourgeois; to fit in takes a husband and family. I didn't want to be always the outsider, the observer.

Thinking over all the countries to live in, I realized that each one had many problems. There was no place where things were "right." Life in California did not seem any better or worse than many places. But for me it was home and a place to make a world.

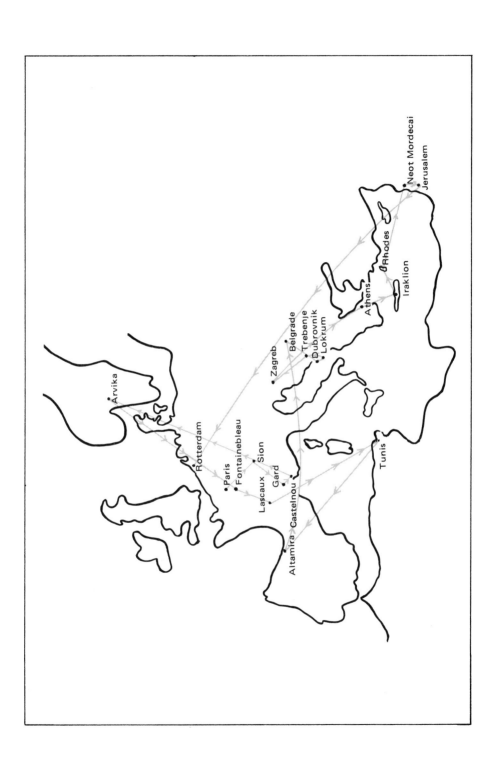

 **mara**
BOOKS

creative art
by **dot Design,** san francisco

The text of this book is set in Linotype Fairfield
by Western Lore Typographers, Los Angeles

Printed and bound by Stecher-Cardoza, San Francisco

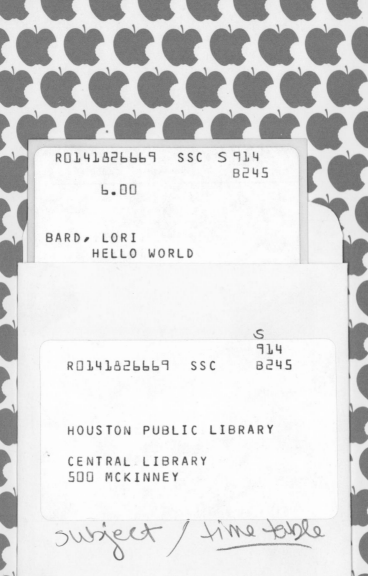
subject / time table

NO circs